Highlights™

Guess Again!

1001 Rib-Tickling Riddles from Highlights

Illustrated by Kevin Rech

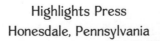

Highlights Press
Honesdale, Pennsylvania

For information about permission to reproduce selections from this book,
please contact permissions@highlights.com.

Published by Highlights for Children, Inc.
P.O. Box 18201
Columbus, Ohio 43218-0201
Distributed to the trade by Boyds Mills Press, Inc.
boydsmillspress.com
Printed in the United States of America

ISBN: 978-1-59078-919-3 $5.95 (PB)

First edition

Visit our website at highlights.com.
10 9 8 7 6 5 4 3 2 1

Design by Barbara Grzeslo
Production by Margaret Mosomillo
The titles are set in Aachen.
The text is set in Bones.

CONTENTS

Wack-a-Doodle Zoo

Where do funny frogs sit?
  On silly pads.

How do you catch a squirrel?
  Climb a tree and act like a nut.

What do you call a monkey
with all his bananas
taken away?

  Furious George.

What do lizards like to eat with their hamburgers?
French flies.

What kind of snake builds houses?
A boa constructor.

Why did the frog cross the road?
Because somebody toad him to.

What's the worst thing you can call a gorilla?
A big baboon.

What do you call a snake that works for the government?
A civil serpent.

What snakes are found on cars?
Windshield vipers.

What do you get if you cross a newborn snake
with a basketball?
   A bouncing baby boa.

What do you call a camel with no hump?

   Humphrey.

What is a frog's favorite drink?
   Croaka-cola.

What is a mole's favorite book?
The digtionary.

What is an ape's favorite cookie?
Chocolate chimp.

What did the worm say to the caterpillar?
"Where did you get that nice fur coat?"

What do polar bears do on the computer?

They surf the winternet.

What lies on its back one hundred feet in the air?
A centipede.

Why can't you tell a joke to a snake?
Because you can't pull its leg.

Why are frogs always happy?
Because they eat whatever bugs them.

How do monkeys go downstairs?
They slide down the bananaster.

Why do birds fly south for the winter?
Because it's too far to walk.

What does a dromedary do when it wants to hide?
It uses camelflage.

What do snakes do after they argue?
They hiss and make up.

What do you call a lazy baby kangaroo?
A pouch potato.

What reptile stays awake at night and sleeps during the day?
A nocturtle.

Why did the crow sit on the telephone wire?
To make a long-distance caw.

What time is it when seven hungry lions are chasing you?
Seven after one.

What kind of bird can you write with?
A penguin.

What do cheetahs like to eat?

Fast food.

Where does a polar bear keep its money?
In a snow bank.

Why did they let the turkey join the band?
Because he had the drumsticks.

What squawks and jumps out of airplanes?
A parrot-trooper.

Who is a penguin's favorite relative?
Auntarctica.

Where do birds stay when they're on vacation?
At a cheep hotel.

What bird never goes to the barber?

A bald eagle.

How do amoebas talk to each other?
With cell phones.

Why won't a teddy bear eat?
Because it's stuffed.

Where do American snakes live?
In the U.SSSSSS.A.

How does a lion greet the other animals on the savannah?
"Pleased to eat you."

When is a well-dressed lion like a weed?
When he's a dandelion.

What animal hates to do laundry?
A leopard, because it has so many spots.

Why did the lion spit out the clown?

Because he tasted funny.

What sound do porcupines make when they kiss?
"Ouch!"

What is small and has big ears and a trunk?
A mouse at summer camp.

What do you get when you cross a snake and
an apple tart?
A piethon.

How do birds see when they're flying in the rain?
They use their wingshield wipers.

What did the buffalo say to his child when he left on a trip?

"Bison."

Why don't cheetahs ever take baths?
Because they don't want to be spotless.

Why didn't the boy trust the tiger?
He thought it was a-lyin'.

How do you stop a skunk from smelling?
You hold its nose.

What do you call a lion at the North Pole?

Lost.

What did the baboon say when he found out his sister had a baby?
"Well, I'll be a monkey's uncle!"

Where does a mouse get a new tail?
At the retail store.

How does a hippopotamus get down from a tree?
It sits on a leaf and waits for the fall.

What kind of pet can't be found at a pet store?
A trumpet.

How does a polar bear build its house?
Igloos it together.

What did the beaver say to the tree?
"It was nice gnawing you!"

What game do mice play?
Hide-and-squeak.

What's worse than a giraffe with a sore throat?
A centipede with athlete's foot.

What did the zookeeper say to his assistants?
"Bear with me!"

What did the seal say to the walrus?
"I'm all fur it!"

What do you get when you cross a caterpillar and a parrot?
A walkie-talkie.

What did the porcupine
say to the cactus?

"Are you my mother?"

What's big and white and lives in the Sahara
Desert?
   A lost polar bear.

How does a horse vote?

He says "yea" or "neigh."

Pretend you are in the jungle and a tiger is
chasing you. What do you do?
   Stop pretending!

Alphabet Bits

Why does Will like the letter W so much?
Because without it he would be ill.

What letter is
always surprised?

G.

What do you call a bear without an ear?
You call it a B.

What do you find in the middle of nowhere?
The letter H.

Which letter is the most difficult to figure out?

Mister E.

How do you spell cat backward?
C-A-T B-A-C-K-W-A-R-D.

How can you spell candy with only two letters?
C and Y.

How do you make one disappear?
Add a G, and it's gone.

What two letters are always jealous?
N V.

What is the longest word?
Smiles. There is a mile between the first and last letters.

What two letters of the alphabet can fly?
B and J.

Is there any word that contains all the vowels?
Unquestionably.

What comes once in a year, never in a month, twice in a week, and never in a day?
The letter E.

Which three letters make everything in the world move?
N R G.

Why is a flower like the letter A?
Because it's followed by a bee.

What five-letter word, when you take away
two letters, is left with one?
Stone.

What starts with T, ends with T, and is full of T?
A teapot.

What starts with an E, ends with an E, and
contains only one letter?
An envelope.

Which three letters would surprise the Invisible
Man?
I C U.

If the alphabet goes from A to Z, what goes from Z to A?

A zebra.

What seven letters did the disappointed boy say when he opened his piggy bank?

"O I C U R M T."

What do you call a person wearing an alphabet suit?

A letter carrier.

Tummy Ticklers

Why did Mr. and Mrs. Tonsil dress up?
   Because the doctor was taking them out.

What do you get if you eat
uranium?

   Atomic ache.

What does a tooth hate to get in the mail?
   A plaque-age.

What did the feet say when they were having fun?

"This is toerific!"

What color can be heard through a wall?

Yellow.

What has two holes, no legs, and runs?

A nose.

Why did the head get so upset?

It was ear-itated.

A boy lost all of his buttons except one. Which one didn't he lose?

His bellybutton.

If grown-ups have knees,
what do children have?

Kid-knees.

What do feet say in the theater?
   "The shoe must go on."

What should you do if you break your arm in
two places?
   Stay away from those places.

What did the left hand say to the other hand?
"How does it feel to always be right?"

How tall is
a person doing
a handstand?

Two feet high.

What is the last thing you take off when you go
to bed?
Your feet (off the floor).

Bugs and Slugs

Why do bees hum?
Because they don't know the words.

What is a caterpillar afraid of?
A dogerpillar.

Why was the little ant confused?
Because all his uncles were ants.

What did the bee say when it was working
very hard?
"I'm buzzy."

How do you find out where a flea has bitten you?
Start from scratch.

Why don't fleas catch cold?
They're always in fur coats.

What's worse than finding a worm in your apple?
Finding half a worm in your apple.

How do slugs begin their fairy tales?

"Once upon a slime . . ."

What do you call a nervous cricket?
  A jitterbug.

What kind of party does a flea go to?
  A fleaesta.

What did one flea say to the other flea?
  "Should we walk or take the dog?"

What did one worm say to the other worm?
  "Where in earth have you been?"

What do you call a traveling flea?
  An itch-hiker.

What kind of bug tells time?
  A clockroach.

What does every tarantula
wish he had?

A hairy godmother.

What vegetable do bugs hate?
  Squash.

There are five flies in the kitchen. Which one is
the cowboy?
  The one on the range.

Why did the spider leave home?
  It wanted to change websites.

How many roaches does it take to screw in a light bulb?

You can't tell. As soon as the light comes on, they scatter.

What do you call a ladybug's husband?

Lord Bug.

What do you call two spiders that just got married?

Newlywebs.

How do bugs make up their minds?
  They pestdecide.

If a moth breathes oxygen in sunlight, what
does it breathe in the dark?
  Nightrogen.

How does a caterpillar start its day?
  It turns over a new leaf.

What do termites do when they need a rest?
  They take a coffee table break.

What do you call a male bug that floats?
  Buoyant.

Why did the fly fly?
  Because the spider spied her.

How do you know which end of a worm is its head?

Tickle the middle and see which end laughs.

What is a spider's favorite picnic food?

Corn on the cobweb.

What happened when two bedbugs fell in love?

They got married in the spring.

What's the best way to prevent infection from biting insects?

Don't bite them.

What did the bee say when it returned to the hive?

"Honey, I'm home!"

What do fireflies say to start a race?
"Ready, set, glow!"

What do you call a cricket that says one thing and does another?
A hypocricket.

What kind of insect can you wear?
A yellow jacket.

What is more amazing
than a talking dog?

A spelling bee.

What is a myth?
A female moth.

When did the bee get married?
When he found his honey.

What goes "zzub, zzub"?
A bee flying backwards.

What does a bug do after it has a cold?
It disinsects its room.

Why do bees itch?
Because they have hives.

What kind of bees are bad at football?
Fumblebees.

What do you call a really big ant?

A giant.

What kind of bee can you throw?
A Frisbee.

Clucks and Yuks

Why did the chicken cross the road?
To prove she wasn't a chicken.

Why did the chickens cross the road?
It seemed like an eggcellent idea.

Why do hens lay eggs?
Because if they dropped them, they'd break.

Which side of a chicken has more feathers?
The outside.

What days do chickens hate most?
Frydays.

What do you have when a pig and a chicken get together for breakfast?

Ham and eggs.

Why did the rooster cross the road?
He wanted to impress the chicks.

Where are chicks born?
  In Chickcago.

Why did the duck cross the road?
  Because it was the chicken's day off.

How does a chicken
tell time?

  One o'cluck, two o'cluck, three o'cluck . . .

Why did the robot cross the road?
  Because the chicken was out of order.

Where do chickens like to sit on a plane?
The wing.

Why did the gum cross the road?
Because it was stuck to the chicken's foot.

What do you get when you cross a chicken and a centipede?
Drumsticks for everyone.

What did the bad chicken lay?
A deviled egg.

Why did the chicken cross the park?
To get to the other slide.

Why did the chicken stop crossing the road?

She was tired of all the chicken jokes.

Why did the chicken stay home from school?
It had the people pox.

Why does a chicken sit on her eggs?
Because she doesn't have a chair.

What did the chicken's fortune cookie say?
"Don't cross the road today—it's bad cluck."

What do chickens put in their gardens?
Eggplants.

Why did the farmer cross the road?
To bring back his chicken.

What do you get when a chicken lays an egg on top of a barn?

An eggroll.

What do you call a dusty chicken that crosses the road and crosses back again?
A dirty double crosser.

Cowabunga!

What is a cow's favorite musical?

The Sound of Moosic.

Why did the cow cross the road?
To get to the udder side.

What did the Triceratops sit on?
Its Tricerabottom.

What's the best way to talk to a Velociraptor?
Long distance.

What kind of dinosaur has no wings, but flies all over?

One that needs a bath.

What do you ask a thirsty tyrannosaur?
  "Tea, Rex?"

What do you call a near-sighted dinosaur?
  Doyathinkhesaurus?

What do you call a near-sighted dinosaur's dog?

Doyouthinkhesaurus Rex.

How can you tell there's a Stegosaurus in your refrigerator?

The door won't close.

What family does Shantungosaurus belong to?

I don't know. No family in our neighborhood has one.

What has a prominent head crest, a duck-like bill, and sixteen wheels?

A Maiasaura on roller skates.

Why did carnivorous dinosaurs eat their meat raw?

Because they didn't know how to barbecue.

What has sharp fangs and sticks to the roof of your mouth?

A peanut butter and Jeholopterus sandwich.

Why didn't dinosaurs drive cars?
Because Tyrannosaurus rex.

Why did the Bambiraptor say "knock, knock?"
Because it was in the wrong joke.

What happened when the dinosaur took the train home?
His mommy made him bring it back.

What dinosaur could jump higher than a house?
All of them—houses can't jump.

How do you season a primordial soup?
With Saltandpepperasaurus.

Why don't dinosaurs ever forget?
Because they never knew anything in the first place.

What do you call a sixty-million-year-old dinosaur?

A fossil.

What did dinosaurs use to make their hot dogs?

Jurassic pork.

What do you say to a ten-ton dinosaur wearing earphones?

Whatever you like—he can't hear you.

Why was the dinosaur afraid to go to the library?

His books were sixty-five million years overdue.

What do you call a sleeping prehistoric reptile?

A dinosnore.

Say "Ahh-ha-ha!"

What did the doctor say to the frog?
"You need a hoperation."

What do you give a sick bird?
Tweetment.

What is the best time to go to the dentist?
Tooth-hurty.

What do you do when your tooth falls out?
Use the toothpaste.

What should you do if your poodle won't stop sneezing?
Call a dogtor.

What do you give a sick relative?
Auntiebiotics.

Where did the soda go when it lost its bubbles?
To the fizzician.

What do you call someone who treats sick ducks?
A ducktor.

What does a doctor do with a sick zeppelin?
She tries to helium.

What makes the tooth fairy so smart?
Wisdom teeth.

What two words in a dentist's office can make a toothache go away?
"You're next."

If an apple a day keeps the doctor away, what does an onion a day do?
It keeps everyone away.

What illness can you catch from a martial-arts expert?
Kung flu.

What did the doctor give the pig for its rash?

Oinkment.

What did one elevator say to the other?
   "I think I'm coming down with something."

What did the ambitious elevator say to his mom?
   "Things are looking up."

What is hairy and coughs?
   A coconut with a cold.

What did the doctor say to the woman who swallowed a spoon?
   "Sit still and don't stir."

What's another name for a dentist's office?
   A filling station.

Why did the cookie go to the doctor?
   It felt crumby.

How does a pig get to the hospital?
In a hambulance.

How do rodents freshen
their breath?

With mousewash.

Tail-Wagging Gags

How do you identify a dog?
Collar I.D.

What did the puppy say when he stepped on sandpaper?
"Rough, rough!"

What kind of dog is made of concrete?
None. I just threw in the concrete to make it hard.

What dog can play football?
A golden receiver.

What animal has the head of a dog, the tail of a dog, and barks like a dog, but isn't a dog?
A puppy.

What did the police dog say to the speeder?
"Stop in the name of the paw!"

When is a dog's tail not a dog's tail?

When it's a wagon.

What do lazy dogs do?
They chase parked cars.

What is the difference between a dog and a flea?
A dog can have fleas, but a flea can't have dogs.

What is a dog's favorite kind of pepper?
Howlapeño.

What kind of dog washes clothes?

A laundromutt.

Where should you never take a dog?
A flea market.

What did the dog say to the car?
  "Hey, you're in my barking spot!"

What does a dog call his father?
  Paw.

How do you know your dog has gotten into the blue paint?
  There are blueprints all over your house.

How does a dogcatcher get paid?
  By the pound.

Which bones do dogs not like?
  Trombones.

How does a dog stop a VCR?
  He presses the paws button.

What do you say to your dogs when they go away?

"Poodle-ooh!"

What did the dog say to the man who pulled his car over to the curb?

"Park! Park!"

What do you call it when your dog sheds all over the couch?

A hairicane.

What do you get if you cross a beagle with bread dough?

Dog biscuits.

Why did the dog learn to tell time?

Because he wanted to be a watchdog.

What kind of dog likes baths?
  A shampoodle.

Why did the Dalmatian go to the eye doctor?

Because he was seeing spots.

What is a dog's favorite movie?
  Jurassic Bark.

What do you call a dog's kiss?
  A pooch smooch.

Kitty City

What works in the circus, meows, and does somersaults?
An acrocat.

What magazine do cats like to read?

Good Mousekeeping.

What do invisible cats drink?
Evaporated milk.

What do you call a cat drinking lemonade?
A sourpuss.

What did the cat say when it stepped on a tack?
"Me-OW!"

Is it bad luck if a black cat follows you?
It depends on whether you're a person or a mouse.

What do you call an eight-sided cat?
An octopuss.

What's another name for a cat's home?
A scratch pad.

What do you call it when it's raining cats?

A downpurr.

What's the difference between a comma and a cat?

   One means "pause at the end of the clause"
   and the other means "claws at the end of
   the paws."

Where do cats go to look at fine art?

The mewseum.

What happened when the cat ate a ball of yarn?
She had mittens.

Ten cats were on a boat. One jumped off. How many were left?

None—they were all copycats.

What do cats say when they want you to open the door?

"Me out."

How do you get a cat to do tricks?

Put a dog in a catsuit.

Where is a cat when the lights go out?

In the dark.

Ele-funnies

Why did the elephant sit on the marshmallow?
Because she didn't want to fall into the cocoa.

Why did the elephant paint her toenails red?
So she could hide in a bowl of cherries.

What's big and gray with horns?
An elephant marching band.

How does an elephant climb a tree?
He stands on an acorn and waits for it to grow.

What does Tarzan say when he sees a herd of elephants?

"Look, a herd of elephants."

What does Tarzan say when he sees a herd of elephants wearing sunglasses?

Nothing—he doesn't recognize them.

What goes down but never goes up?

An elephant in an elevator.

What do you get when you cross an elephant with a parrot?

An animal that tells you everything it remembers.

If there were two elephants under one umbrella, why didn't they get wet?

It wasn't raining.

What do you call an elephant in a phone booth?

Stuck.

Why do elephants have wrinkles?
Ever tried to iron an elephant?

What did the grape say when the elephant stepped on him?
Nothing—he just let out a little wine.

How do you fit four elephants in a red Mini?
Two in the front and two in the back.

How do you know there is an elephant in your refrigerator?
There are footprints in the butter.

How do you know there are two elephants in your fridge?
You can hear them talking.

How do you know there are three elephants in your fridge?

You can't close the door.

How do you know there are four elephants in your fridge?

There's a red Mini in your driveway.

Why is an elephant like a car and a tree?

They all have trunks.

What time is it when an elephant sits on your fence?

Time to get a new fence.

What did the elephant do when he stubbed his toe?

He called a toe truck.

Why do ducks have webbed feet?

To stomp out forest fires.

Why do elephants have large feet?
To stomp out flaming ducks.

What do you get when you cross a kangaroo
with an elephant?
Great big holes all over Australia.

How are an elephant and a grape alike?
They're both purple, except for the elephant.

Why did the elephant wear green sneakers?
Because his red ones were in the wash.

Why did the elephant float down the river on
his back?
To keep his sneakers dry.

What do you call an elephant with wings?
A jumbo jet.

What is beautiful, gray, and wears glass slippers?
Cinderelephant.

How do you scold an elephant?
"Tusk, tusk."

How do you hunt for elephants?
Hide in a bush and make a noise like a peanut.

What is as big as an elephant, yet weighs nothing?

An elephant's shadow.

Why doesn't the elephant use the computer?

It's afraid of the mouse.

Why can't two elephants swim at the same time?

Because they have only one pair of trunks.

Why do elephants have trunks?
They'd look pretty silly with glove compartments.

Why is an elephant big, gray, and wrinkly?
Because if it was small, white, and smooth it would be an aspirin.

Comical Acres

How did the farmer fix his jeans?
With a cabbage patch.

What kind of pictures do sheep like to paint?

Lambscapes.

What do you call a duck with a big bill?
Poor.

Why can't you tell a secret in a cornfield?
There are too many ears.

What did the apple tree say to the farmer?
"Quit picking on me."

Why did the pig want to be an actor?

He was a big ham.

What animal always sleeps with its shoes on?
  A horse.

What does a farmer do when his sheep are hurt?
  He calls a lambulance.

Why did the sheep keep going straight down
the street?
  No ewe turns were allowed.

Why did the farmer throw vegetables on the
ground?
  He wanted peas on Earth.

What kind of jokes do farmers tell?
  Corny ones.

What has four legs and flies?
A horse in the summertime.

What happens when a pig loses its voice?
It becomes disgruntled.

Where do sheep go to get their hair cut?
To the baa baa shop.

How does a hog write a letter?

With a pigpen.

What happened when the pigpen broke?
The pig used a pencil.

How do you make a turkey float?
*With two scoops of ice cream, a bottle of
root beer, and a turkey.*

What was the worm doing in the cornfield?
Going in one ear and out the other.

Where did the first corn come from?
The stalk brought it.

How do you fit more pigs on your farm?
Build a styscraper.

Who stole the soap?
The robber ducky.

Why did the farmer plant money in her garden?
She wanted rich soil.

When did the duck wake up this morning?

At the quack of dawn.

Why did the farmer call her pig Ink?
It kept running out of its pen.

What do you put on a bad pig?
Hamcuffs.

What do you call the father of an ear of corn?
Popcorn.

What did the mare say when she finished her hay?
"That's the last straw."

What do you call a teeter-totter for donkeys?
A hee-haw see-saw.

What do horses put on their burgers?
Mayoneighs.

What do you call a royal horse?
His Majesteed.

Where does a sheep like to stand in line?
At the baaaack.

What kind of vegetables do you pick in the winter?

Snow peas.

What kind of machine raises pigs?

A porklift.

What do you call a sleeping bull?

A bulldozer.

Why did the sheep jump over the moon?
Because the cow was on vacation.

Why do sheep dislike crowds?
They're very baaaashful.

What do flowers say when they explode?
"Ka-bloooom!"

What do horses do at bedtime?
They hit the hay.

What is the definition of a farmer?
Someone who is outstanding in his field.

How do sheep carry their homework?
In baaaackpacks.

What do you call a line of rabbits walking backward?

A receding hare line.

Cutup Cuisine

What is the laziest food ever?
Bread—it just loafs around.

What is a camera's favorite kind of sandwich?
Cheese.

What is green and goes "slam, slam, slam, slam"?
A four-door pickle.

What did the butter say to the brake?
"Why did you stop? I was on a roll."

What dip do bath towels eat at parties?
Shower cream and onion.

What is dinner's favorite sport?
Biscuitball.

How do you make hot dogs shiver?
Put chili beans on them.

What is a mushroom's favorite vacation spot?

Port-a-Bella.

What is brown, greasy, and lives in a tower?
The lunch bag of Notre Dame.

In mathematics, what is the law of the doughnut?

Two halves make a hole.

What happens when you tell an egg a great joke?
It totally cracks up.

What did the nut say when it sneezed?
  "Cashew!"

Would Little Miss Muffet share her curds?
  No whey!

Would Little Miss Muffet share her whey?
  Of curds she would!

What do you get if you drop a basket of fruit?
  Fruit salad.

How do you make a hot dog stand?
  Take away its chair.

Why did the woman wear a helmet at the dinner table?
  She was on a crash diet.

What does a sweet potato wear to bed?
Its yammies.

What kind of nut doesn't have a shell?
A doughnut.

What is the best thing to put in a pie?
Your teeth.

What is the best time to eat a banana?
When the moment is ripe.

What do bakers put on their beds?
Cookie sheets.

What did one potato chip say to the other potato chip?
"Want to go for a dip?"

What do vegetables read with their coffee?
  Newspeppers.

What did the cook name his son?
  Stew.

Why should you knock
before you open
the refrigerator?

Because you might see the salad dressing.

How did the calendar survive on a desert
island?
  It ate the dates.

What do you call a shivering glass of milk?
A milkshake.

What did the hamburger name its daughter?
Patty.

Why couldn't the egg lend his friend money?
Because he was broke.

What is yellow and writes?
A ballpoint banana.

What kind of candy is always tardy?
Chocolate.

What did the ear of corn say when it was
about to be peeled?
"Shucks."

Why was the banana so popular?
It had a peel.

Why is bread lots of fun?
It's made of wheeeat.

Where do hamburgers dance?
At a meatball.

What do beavers eat for breakfast?

Oakmeal.

What is a clown's favorite snack?
Peanut riddle.

What do chess players have for breakfast?
Pawncakes.

How do you make an egg roll?
You push it.

How do you fix a broken pizza?
With tomato paste.

What is a tree's favorite drink?
Root beer.

What side dish does a miner eat?
Coal slaw.

What do you get when you cross a watermelon with a bus?

A fruit that can seat forty-five people.

Why did the banana go to the doctor?

Because it wasn't peeling well.

Why can't you feed a teddy bear?

Because it's already stuffed.

What do you call a banana with wings?

A fruit fly.

What cheese is made backward?

Edam.

What has eyes but can't see?

A potato.

What do you give to a puppy that has a fever?

Mustard—it's the best thing for a hot dog.

What did the banana do when it heard the ice cream?
    It split.

What kind of room has no doors, no windows, and no walls?
    A mushroom.

Why didn't the hot dog star in the movies?
  The rolls weren't good enough.

How do you know that carrots are good for
your eyes?

Have you ever seen a rabbit wearing glasses?

What is a boxer's favorite drink?
  Fruit punch.

What did the syrup say to its long-lost friend?
  "It's been a waffle long time!"

Why did the orange use sunblock?
Because it was starting to peel.

What do you call rotten eggs, rotten fruit, and spoiled milk in a bag?
Grosseries.

How do you turn soup into gold?
You add twenty-four carrots.

How do you make a strawberry shake?
By taking it to a scary movie.

What is a tortilla chip's favorite kind of dance?
Salsa.

What kind of tables do people eat?
Vegetables.

Why did the cookie cry?
  His mom had been a wafer so long.

How do clowns like their eggs?

Funny-side up.

Why was the little apple so excited?
  He was going to see his Granny Smith.

Why don't bananas snore?
Because they don't want to wake the rest of the bunch.

What do you get when you cross a banana with a knife?
A banana split.

What is the most adorable vegetable?
The cutecumber.

Why did the bacon laugh?
Because the egg cracked a yolk.

What does a cookie say when it's excited?
"Chip, chip, hooray!"

How did the egg cross the road?
   It scrambled.

Why is a giraffe a bad dinner guest?

It eats, leaves.

Geography Gigglers

If Mississippi gave Missouri her New Jersey,
what would Delaware?
I don't know, but Alaska.

Which country's name is a verb?
Togo.

Where does bacteria go on vacation?
Germany.

What should you do when you find Chicago, IL?
Call Baltimore, MD.

Why is the Mississippi such an unusual river?
Because it has four eyes and can't see.

Which city always needs a compass?
Lost Angeles.

What did Tennessee?

The same thing that Arkansas.

What's the greatest engineering feat performed in the US?
Wheeling West Virginia.

What is the greatest surgical operation ever recorded?

Lansing Michigan.

What did the mom volcano say to the kid volcano?

"I lava you."

How does a lump of coal start a story?

"Once upon a mine . . ."

What do volcanoes eat for dinner?

Lavacados.

Why won't the hills play hide-and-seek with the mountains?

Because the mountains peak.

Where are the Great Plains?
At the great airports.

What city has no buildings or people?
Electricity.

Why did Milly spill the glass of water?
Because she wanted to see the waterfall.

Why did the river go on a diet?
It had gained a few ponds.

What's yellow and always points north?
A magnetic banana.

What did one mountain say to the other
mountain?
"Meet me in the valley."

Who is married to Antarctica?
   Uncle Arctica.

What is the best thing to take into the desert?
   A thirst-aid kit.

Why is Alabama
the smartest state
in the USA?

Because it has four A's and one B.

What travels around the world yet never leaves
its corner?
   A stamp.

What is the capital of Washington?
  The W.

What has cities without houses, rivers without water, and forests without trees?
  A map.

What is the capital of Alaska?
  Come on—Juneau this one!

What rock group has four men that don't sing?
  Mount Rushmore.

What is the fastest country in the world?
  Russia.

What do you call a snowman in Florida?
  Water.

What state do horses and lions like best?
Maine.

What state is round on the sides and high in the middle?
Ohio.

What is a rodent's favorite city?
Hamsterdam.

Where do shoelaces go on vacation?
Thailand.

What did one volcano say to the other volcano?
"Stop interupting me!"

Which is the best state for a wedding?
Maryland.

What is a snake's favorite river?
  The Hississippi.

Who sells ice cream in Arizona?

The Good Yuma man.

Weirdly Witty

What is a witch's favorite subject?
Spelling.

What did the wizard say to his girlfriend?
"You look wanderful tonight."

What did one ghost say to the other ghost?
"Do you believe in people?"

Why did Frankenstein's monster like the
stand-up comic?
Because she kept him in stitches.

How do you greet a French skeleton?
"Bonjour."

What do vampires put on their holiday turkey?
Gravey.

Who is the best dancer at a Halloween party?
The boogieman.

Why did Dracula go to the doctor?

He was coffin.

What do monsters put on before they go in the pool?
Sunscream.

What does a ghost put on its bagel?
Scream cheese.

Where do you find the most famous dragons?
In the Hall of Flame.

Why couldn't the skeleton go to the party?
He had nobody to go with.

How do monsters tell their futures?
They read their horrorscopes.

What is a vampire's favorite holiday?
Fangsgiving.

Why did the girl take a bale of hay to bed with her?

To feed her nightmare.

Where do ghosts go for a vacation?

The Boohamas.

How many witches does it take to change a light bulb?

Just one, but she changes it into a toad.

Why did the boy carry a clock and a bird on Halloween?

He was going tick-or-tweeting.

What do you call a fairy that needs a bath?

Stinkerbell.

What is a goblin's favorite ride at the amusement park?
The roller ghoster.

Why did the monster need braces?

Because he had an ogre bite.

Where do witches get their hair done?
The ugly parlor.

What is a skeleton's favorite instrument?
A trombone.

What is Dracula's favorite coffee?

Decoffinated.

What do ghosts eat for breakfast?
Scream of wheat.

What do Hawaiian pumpkins say?
"Happy Hulaween!"

What does a witch request at a hotel?
Broom service.

How do witches tell the time?
By looking at their witchwatches.

What do you call a ghost's mother and father?
Transparents.

What would you get if you crossed a snowball
with a vampire?
Frostbite.

What is a monster's favorite game?
Swallow the leader.

Which kind of ghost haunts a chicken coop?

A poultrygeist.

What do baby ghosts wear on their feet?
Booties.

What's a vampire's favorite dance?
The fangdango.

What do you call a skeleton that is always telling lies?
A bony phony.

What do you call a giant mummy?
Gauzilla.

What do you call a prehistoric ghost?
A terrordactyl.

What kind of ghost has the best hearing?
The eeriest.

Why don't skeletons play music in church?
They have no organs.

What do ghosts have in the seats of their cars?
Sheet belts.

How do skeletons get their mail?
By bony express.

Why did the vampire give up acting?
He couldn't sink his teeth into the part.

What happened when the werewolf swallowed a clock?
He got ticks.

What do you get if you cross Dracula and Al Capone?
A fangster.

What kind of jewels do ghosts wear?
Tombstones.

What do ghosts eat for dinner?
Ghoulash.

What do you call a skeleton snake?
A rattler.

What does a vampire stand on after taking a shower?
A bat mat.

What is a ghost's favorite day of the week?
Frightday.

What goes "cackle, cackle, bonk"?
A witch laughing her head off.

Which Halloween character eats the fastest?
The goblin.

What do you get if you cross a witch and an iceberg?
A cold spell.

What does a witch's cat like for breakfast?
Mice crispies.

What do you call a witch who likes the beach but is scared of the water?
A chicken sandwitch.

What is the difference between a witch and the letters M-A-K-E-S?
One makes spells and the others spell makes.

Why didn't the witch sing at the concert?
Because she had a frog in her throat.

What do you call a hairy beast that is lost?

A wherewolf.

Why did the vampire keep falling for the oldest tricks in the book?
Because he's a sucker.

What kind of tests do they give in witch school?
Hexaminations.

Who turns the lights off on Halloween?
The light's witch.

What do you call a wizard from outer space?
A flying sorcerer.

What is a ghost's favorite sandwich?
Booloney.

When do Halloween monsters eat their candy?
On Chewsday.

Why are graveyards so noisy?
Because of all the coffin.

Why is Halloween so fun for ghouls?
Because Halloween is a ghoul's best friend.

Why are skeletons so calm, cool, and collected?
Because nothing gets under their skin.

What kind of horse does the boogeyman ride?
A nightmare.

What's the best game to play at Halloween?
Hide and shriek.

What's the only music a Halloween mummy
listens to?
Wrap.

Why don't skeletons work as stunt men?
They don't have the guts.

What do ghosts do at garage sales?
  They go bargain haunting.

What do witches love about their computers?

The spell checker.

Why did the witch put her broom in the washing machine?
  She wanted a clean sweep.

What do you call a pumpkin that thinks it's a comedian?

A joke-o'-lantern.

What did the people say when the goo monsters attacked?

"Ooze going to save us?"

What sound does a witch's cereal make?

Snap, cackle, and pop.

What do you get if you cross a dinosaur with a wizard?

Tyrannosaurus hex.

Why do ghosts make good cheerleaders?

Because they have spirit.

Why did the skeleton go to the barbecue pit?
To get a sparerib.

What is a ghoul's favorite cheese?
Monsterella.

What's the best way to talk to a monster?
Long distance.

Why don't vampires have any friends?
Because they're a pain in the neck.

Hilarious History

How do you find King Arthur in the dark?
With a knight light.

What do you call an
American drawing?

A Yankee doodle.

How many ears did Davy Crockett have?
Three—a left ear, a right ear, and a wild frontier.

How did Noah see at night on the ark?
Floodlights.

What is a forum?
Two-um plus two-um.

How did Columbus's men sleep on their ships?
With their eyes shut.

Who built the ark?
I have Noah idea.

How did the Vikings send secret messages?
By Norse code.

Who succeeded the first president of the United States?
The second one.

What did they do at the Boston Tea Party?
I don't know—I wasn't invited.

What do you get
if you cross a
US president
with a shark?

Jaws Washington.

Where were English kings usually crowned?
On the head.

Why does the Statue of Liberty stand in
New York harbor?
Because it can't sit down.

Why were the early days of history called the
Dark Ages?
Because there were so many knights.

What did George Washington say to his men
before they got into the boat?
"Get in the boat, men."

What did Mason say to Dixon?
"We've got to draw the line here."

Why aren't you doing well in history?
Because the teacher keeps asking about things that happened before I was born.

What did Paul Revere say when his ride was over?
"Whoa!"

Which American president wore the largest hat?
The one with the biggest head.

Where did people dance in medieval times?
In knight clubs.

Where was the Declaration of Independence signed?
At the bottom.

What do Alexander the Great and Winnie the Pooh have in common?

They have the same middle name.

Which president was the most environmentally aware?

Treeodore Roosevelt.

What does the president hang in the White House on the Fourth of July?

The Decoration of Independence.

What was Camelot?

A place to park camels.

Homegrown Humor

Why did the dust bunny use the computer?
To go on the linternet.

What did the bald man say when he got a comb for his birthday?

"Thanks, I'll never part with it."

What did the boy use to keep track of his mother?

A thermometer.

What did the picture say to the wall?

"I've got you covered."

What did the sandal say to the sneaker?

"Don't stick your tongue out at me!"

What has a foot on each side and one in the middle?

A yardstick.

What is full of holes but can still hold water?

A sponge.

What do chairs use to hold up their pants?

Seat belts.

How did the grandmother knit a suit of armor?

She used steel wool.

When is a door not a door?
When it's ajar.

What is a door's favorite kind of joke?
A knock-knock.

What has teeth but can't eat?
   A comb.

What do you go in and out of that spins and makes you feel calmer?
   A resolving door.

What did the happy light bulb say to the sad light bulb?
   "Why don't you lighten up?"

What can go up a chimney down but can't go down a chimney up?
   An umbrella.

What did the tie say to the hat?
   "You go on ahead and I'll hang around."

What does one clock say to another clock on its birthday?
    "You're getting older by the minute."

What did the carpet say to the ceiling?
    "I look up to you."

What kind of clothing does a house wear?

An address.

What does a broom do when it's tired?
It goes to sweep.

Where do books sleep?
Under their covers.

What is bought by the yard and worn by the foot?
A carpet.

Where can everyone find money?
In the dictionary.

What does an expensive TV have in common with a dictionary on top of a mountain?
They're both high definition.

What gets wetter the more it dries?
A towel.

Why did the boy put cheese beside the computer?
To feed the mouse.

Why did the computer cross the road?
It wanted to get with the program.

What did one wall say to the other wall?
"Meet you at the corner."

What did one camera say to the other when it saw something interesting?
"That's flashinating."

What did one candle say to the other candle?
"Are you going out tonight?"

What did the lamp say to the chandelier?
"What are you hanging around for?"

What kind of pen
wears a wig?

A baldpoint.

Who can jump higher than a house?
Everyone—houses can't jump.

What's the best side of the house to put
the porch on?
The outside.

What do snakes put on their kitchen floors?
Reptiles.

What did the digital clock say to the grandfather clock?
"Look, Grandpa—no hands!"

What's another name for a grandfather clock?

An old-timer.

Laugh Logic

What word in the English language is
pronounced wrong, even by scholars?
Wrong.

How many months have twenty-eight days?
All of them.

What gets colder as it warms up?
An air conditioner.

What is three quarters of one million dollars?
Seventy-five cents.

Which candle burns longer—a blue candle or a red candle?

Neither. They both burn shorter.

The red house is on the white street, and the blue house is on the red street. Where is the white house?

Washington, DC.

How many men were born in 1996?

No men were born—only babies.

How many knees does a person have?
Four: a left knee, a right knee, and two kidneys.

Which building has the most stories?
The library.

Which is faster—hot or cold?
Hot, because you can catch a cold.

If Washington went to Washington wearing white woollies while Washington's wife waited in Wilmington, how many W's are there in all?
There are no W's in all.

Which is better: an old ten-dollar bill or a new one?
An old ten-dollar bill, because a new one is worth only one dollar.

What belongs to you but is used mostly by other people?
Your name.

How is it possible for Sarah to be in fourth grade for twenty-seven years?
She teaches fourth grade.

What is easy to get into but hard to get out of?
Trouble.

Is it correct to say "The yolk of the egg is white" or "The yolk of the egg are white"?
Neither is correct—the yolk is yellow.

What goes all the way around the world but never moves an inch?
The equator.

There is an electric train traveling north. Suddenly it turns around and goes south. Which way does the steam go?

It's an electric train—it doesn't have steam.

What is harder to catch the faster you run?

Your breath.

A cowboy rides into town on Friday. He stays three days, then leaves on Friday. How does he do it?

His horse's name is Friday.

What is cut and spread out on a table but never eaten?

A deck of cards.

What can't the strongest man hold for a quarter of an hour?

His breath.

What is yesterday's tomorrow and tomorrow's yesterday?

Today.

What breaks but never falls and what falls but never breaks?

Dawn breaks without falling, and night falls without breaking.

Why can't you go more than halfway into the woods?

Because then you'd be going out.

Two fathers and two sons order three hamburgers. Each person gets a hamburger. How?

There are only three people: a grandfather, a father, and a son.

How can you go without sleep for seven days?

Sleep at night.

What is dark but made by light?

A shadow.

Tom said, "I was seven years old on my last birthday, and I will be nine years old on my next birthday." How can this be true?

Tom turned eight today.

What's the difference between a smart aleck and a man's question?

One is a wise guy, and the other is a guy's why.

What is black when you buy it, red when you use it, and gray when you throw it away?

Coal.

What falls day after day but never hits the ground?

Night.

What roars but doesn't have a mouth?

A fire.

What is the difference between a postage stamp and a girl?

One is a mail fee and the other is a female.

What's the difference between the law and an ice cube?

One is justice, and the other is just ice.

What do you call a millionaire who never takes a shower?

Filthy rich.

What runs but never walks?
  Water.

The clerk at the butcher shop is five feet ten inches tall and wears size thirteen sneakers. What does he weigh?

Meat.

Before Mt. Everest was discovered, what was the highest mountain in the world?

Mt. Everest—it just wasn't discovered yet.

Johnny's mother had three children. The first child was named April. The second child was named May. What was the third child's name?

Johnny.

How much dirt is there in a hole that measures two feet by three feet by four feet?

There is no dirt in a hole.

What is the best cure for insomnia?

A good night's sleep.

Michelle was born on December 28, yet her birthday is always in the summer. How is this possible?

Michelle lives in the Southern Hemisphere.

If you were running a race, and you passed the person in second place, what place would you be in?

You would be in second; you passed the person in second place, not first.

If a farmer has five haystacks in one field and four haystacks in the other field, how many haystacks would he have if he combined them all in another field?

One big stack.

What word in the English language is always spelled incorrectly?

Incorrectly.

Life is tough, but what can you always count on?

Your fingers.

What is at the end of a rainbow?
  The letter W.

How do you buy time?
  Purchase a watch.

What has two hands but can't clap?
  A clock.

What goes around a field but does not move?
  A fence.

What kind of bow can't be tied?
  A rainbow.

What runs through the city without moving?
  A road.

What did the teapot say to the chalk?
  Nothing—teapots can't talk.

What goes up and never comes down?
  Your age.

What's a thing, but not a thing at all?
  Nothing.

What has a face that can't see and hands that can't hold?
  A clock.

What gets lots of answers but no questions?
  A doorbell.

What has a head and tail, but no body?
  A coin.

What are the strongest days of the week?
Saturday and Sunday; the rest are weekdays.

Why did the boy put a ruler next to his bed?

Because he wanted to see how long he slept.

What can you break using only your mouth?
Silence.

What's at the beginning of eternity, the end of time and space, the beginning of every end, and the end of every race?
The letter E.

The more you take of these, the more you leave. What are they?
Footsteps.

What has five (sometimes four) hands, but is normal?
A man carrying a grandfather clock.

You walk into a room with a fireplace, a wood stove, and a kerosene lamp. You have only one match. What do you light first?
The match.

Why can't you take a picture of a man with a hat?
Because you can't take a picture with a hat.

What can you put in a barrel to make it lighter?
A hole.

Do, Re, Mi, Whee!

What do playing the piano and running too fast have in common?

If you don't C sharp, you will B flat.

What is an elf's favorite music?

Gift rap.

Which instrument never tells the truth?
A lyre.

What is hair's least favorite dance?
The tangle.

What do you get if you cross a mummy with a CD?
A wrap.

What is Tarzan's favorite Christmas carol?
"Jungle Bells."

What kind of music do hammocks like?
Rock.

What is a rock star's favorite food?
Jam.

What is a detective's favorite dance?
The evidance.

What kind of music do they play on a space shuttle?
Rocket roll.

What do you call singing in the shower?

A soap opera.

What kind of music did the Pilgrims like?
Plymouth Rock.

Why did the robot win the dance contest?
He was a dancing machine.

Why did people dance when the vegetable band played?
The music had a good beet.

If you are in a room with no windows, a locked door, and a piano, what do you do?
Use a piano key to unlock the door.

What kind of music do bubbles hate?
Pop.

What kind of music do rabbits like?
Hip-hop.

What is a bumblebee's least favorite musical note?
B flat.

What did the conductor say to the orchestra?
"We've got a score to settle."

What is a woodwind player's favorite dessert?
Flutecake.

What does a musician brush his teeth with?
A tuba toothpaste.

Why did the music teacher need a ladder?
To reach the high notes.

What kind of meat do singers like to eat?
So-la-mi.

What is a musical note's favorite sport?
Beat boxing.

What's green and sings?

Elvis Parsley.

What is a trombone's favorite thing on the playground?
The slide.

If lightning strikes an orchestra, who is most likely to get hit?
The conductor.

What does a cow play?

Moo-sic.

Fun by the Numbers

Why was 6 mad at 7?
Because 7 8 9.

Why is 2+2=5 like your left foot?
It's not right.

What did one math book say to the other?
"We've got problems."

What did one calculator say to the other?
"You can count on me."

Why is it dangerous to do math in the jungle?
Because when you add four and four you get ate.

What is a math teacher's favorite dessert?
Pi.

What tools do you need for math?
Multipliers.

What did the math classroom have instead of desks?
Times tables.

Where do New York City kids learn their multiplication tables?
Times Square.

What has wings and solves number problems?
A mothematician.

Why is arithmetic hard work?

You have to carry all those numerals.

What did the zero say to the eight?
"Nice belt."

Why is a circle always hot?
Because it is 360 degrees.

How many feet are in a yard?
That depends on how many people are standing in it.

Which Mexican food is like a ruler?
An inchilada.

What grew from the plant in the math room?
Square roots.

How do you make seven even?
Take away the letter S.

What time is it when the clock strikes thirteen?
Time to fix the clock.

What kind of numbers hide in the grass?
Arithmeticks.

If two is a couple and three's a crowd, what are four and five?
Nine.

When Mel has six piñon nuts and Melanie has seven piñon nuts, what do they have?
A difference of a piñon.

Jollies on the Job

Why do ballerinas wear tutus?
Three-threes are too big and one-ones are too small.

Why was the scientist's head wet?
Because he had a brainstorm.

Why do barbers get there sooner?
Because they know all the shortcuts.

What did the painter say after he spilled paint on the boy?
"Are you all white?"

What is a banker's favorite dance?
The vaults.

What did the judge say when a skunk walked into his courtroom?

"Odor in the court!"

Why do firemen wear red suspenders?
To hold up their pants.

Where do generals keep their armies?
In their sleevies.

Why did the detective carry a flashlight?
To shed some light on the case.

What do you call a lawyer's house?
A legal pad.

What do you call an ice-cream truck operator?
A sundae driver.

What does the president do when he has a
toothache?
He makes a presidential appointment.

What do you call a man who's always wiring for money?

An electrician.

What did the limestone say to the geologist?

"Don't take me for granite."

How much does a pirate pay to get his ears pierced?

A buccaneer.

What happened when the jester fell in the pond?

He got joking wet.

What do artists use when they are sleepy?
    Crayawns.

Where does a lumberjack go to buy things?
    The chopping center.

What's another name for a mobile-home salesman?
    A wheel-estate dealer.

Who never gets paid for a day's work?
    A night watchman.

Where do scientists read facts about volcanoes?
    In magmazines.

What do police officers put on their bread?
    Traffic jam.

What did the painting say to the detective?
"It wasn't me—I was framed!"

Why did the ice-cream cone join the newspaper?
To get the latest scoop.

What did the detective say when he shut his briefcase?
"Case closed!"

Why did the comedian go out of business?
His jokes didn't make any cents.

Why did the banker freeze his money?
He wanted cold, hard cash.

Where do superheros shop?

At the supermarket.

What do you need to know if you want to be
a lion tamer?
 More than the lion.

Why did the superhero save the pickle?
 Because he wanted to eat it later.

Where do explorers go to play?
 A jungle gym.

What do you call a man who shaves twenty times a day?
   A barber.

Why did the police officer wear his bed sheets to work?
   He was working undercover.

Cosmic Chuckles

What did the astronomer do when his theory
was proved correct?
He thanked his lucky stars.

What do astronauts use to keep their pants up?
Asteroid belts.

What do you say to a two-headed space alien?
"Hello, hello!"

Why didn't the rocket have a job?
Because it was fired.

What is big and red and eats rocks?
A big red rock eater.

Why are E.T.'s eyes so big?
Yours would be too if you saw his phone bill.

What does one star say to another star when they pass by?
"Glad to meteor."

What holds the sun up in the sky?
Sunbeams.

How does the man in the moon get his hair cut?
Eclipse it.

Where do astronauts go to study?
The mooniversity.

How do you have a good outer space party?
Planet.

What happens when an astronaut lets go of his sundae?
He gets an ice-cream float.

Why does the moon go to the bank?
To change quarters.

What does Saturn like to read?
Comet books.

Why should you never insult a Martian?
It might get its feelers hurt.

How did Mary's little lamb get to Mars?
By rocket sheep.

If athletes get athlete's foot, what do astronauts get?

Missile toe.

What do space aliens eat for breakfast?

Flying sausages.

What sound does a space turkey make?
"Hubble, hubble, hubble."

How is food served in space?
In satellite dishes.

What are the solar system's three favorite days
of the week?
Saturnday, Sunday, and Moonday.

What did the dentist call the astronaut's cavity?
A black hole.

Why is Saturn like a jewelry box?
Because it has rings.

Where do aliens keep their coffee cups?
On flying saucers.

What type of knot do you tie in outer space?
An astroknot.

Where do astronauts store their food?
In launch boxes.

How does an alien count to twenty-three?
On its fingers.

Why did the moon stop eating?
It was full.

LOL Lessons

What did the glue say to the teacher?
"I'm stuck on you."

Why did the boy eat his homework?

Because the teacher said it was a piece of cake.

Why did the clock in the cafeteria always
run slow?
Every lunch it went back four seconds.

Why was the karate teacher arrested at the
butcher shop?
He was caught choplifting.

What do you do if a teacher rolls her eyes at you?
Pick them up and roll them back to her.

What flies around the kindergarten room at night?
The alphabat.

Why did the student bring scissors to school?
He wanted to cut class.

What is king of the classroom?
The ruler.

Why are school cafeteria workers so mean?
Because they batter fish, beat eggs, and whip cream.

Why couldn't the music teacher open his classroom door?

Because his keys were on the piano.

What do you call a boy with a dictionary in his pocket?
Smartypants.

Why did the teacher draw on the window?
Because he wanted his lesson to be clear.

What's the difference between a teacher and a train?
The teacher says, "Spit out your gum," and the train says, "Choo-choo."

What did the student say after the teacher said, "Order in the classroom"?
"I'll have a burger and fries, please."

Where did the pencil go for vacation?
To Pennsylvania.

Why did the new boy steal a chair from the classroom?
Because the teacher told him to take a seat.

When is a blue schoolbook not a blue schoolbook?
When it is read.

What's the worst thing that can happen to a geography teacher?
Getting lost.

How do you get straight A's?
By using a ruler.

What did the pen say to the pencil?
"So, what's your point?"

What's the best place to grow flowers in school?
In kindergarten.

Why did the clock go to the principal's office?
For tocking too much.

What happened when the teacher tied all the kids' shoelaces together?
They had a class trip.

Why was the child's report card all wet?

Because it was under C-level.

Why did the teacher go to the beach?
To test the water.

What does a fairy like to sing at school?
The elfabet song.

Why should you never dot another student's i's?
*You should always keep your i's on your
own paper.*

What do elves do after school?
Gnomework.

What do you get when you put the letters M
and T together?

Nothing—it's empty!

What do baby bunnies learn in school?
The alfalfabet.

How do bees get to school?
They take the school buzz.

What topping do teachers put on their pizza?
Graded cheese.

What kind of dance do teachers like best?
Attendance.

What would you get if you crossed a vampire and a teacher?
Lots of blood tests.

What school did the alphabet go to?
LMNtary.

Why does the sun seem so bright?
Because it shines in class.

What do teachers like to eat while writing on the blackboard?
Chalklates.

What do you call a duck that gets all A's in school?
A wise quacker.

When does a teacher carry birdseed?
When she has a parrot-teacher conference.

What did the glue say to the paper?
"Let's stick together."

What has forty feet and sings?
The school choir.

What coin can you write with?
A penny.

What sheds its skin but isn't alive?
An eraser.

Why is an ice cube so smart?

It has thirty-two degrees.

What subject do owls like to study?
Owlgebra.

What is root beer's favorite subject?
Fizzics.

What did the mom chameleon say to her nervous kid on the first day of school?
"Don't worry, you'll blend right in!"

Seagoing Sillies

Why are fish so smart?
Because they live in schools.

What lives in the sea and carries a lot of people?

An octobus.

Why does the ocean roar?
You would, too, if you had lobsters in your bed.

What kind of fish likes bubble gum?

A blowfish.

Why do sea gulls fly over the sea?
Because if they flew over the bay, they would be bagels.

What fish is the most valuable?
The goldfish.

What fish comes out at night?
A starfish.

Who was the first underwater spy?
James Pond.

What's the difference between a fish and a piano?
You can't tuna fish.

What do you call a frightened skin diver?
A chicken of the sea.

What do fish do when they are bored?
Watch telefishion.

Where do boats go when they are sick?
To the dock.

What did the boy octopus say to the girl octopus?

"I want to hold your hand, hand, hand, hand, hand, hand, hand, hand."

Why wouldn't the fish watch TV?

He was afraid he'd get hooked.

What did the fish give to his teacher?

A crab apple.

Who eats at underwater restaurants?

Scuba diners.

Why are fish such poor tennis players?

They're afraid of the net.

What do you call a clam that doesn't share?

A selfish shellfish.

What is the best way to catch a fish?
Have someone throw it to you.

What does a sea monster eat for dinner?

Fish and ships.

How do you divide the sea in half?
With a sea saw.

What's wet and says, "How do you do?" sixteen times?

Two octopuses shaking hands.

Why do opera singers make good sailors?

They know how to handle high C's.

What do you call a fish with no eyes?

A fsh.

What lives in the ocean and always agrees with you?

A seal of approval.

What is the best way to get around the ocean floor?

By taxi crab.

What do you call a big fish that makes you an offer you can't refuse?

The Codfather.

What is an oyster's strongest friend?

A mussel.

What did the boy get when he leaned over the back of the boat?

A stern warning.

What do you do with a blue whale?
Cheer it up.

What happened to the eel that got loose in the mall?
It went on a shocking spree.

What vitamin do fish take?
Vitamin sea.

What did the sea otter have for lunch?
Abalone sandwich.

What is the best way to communicate with a fish?
Drop it a line.

What seafood goes well with peanut butter?
Jellyfish.

What do you get when you cross a school of fish with a herd of elephants?
Swimming trunks.

What can make an octopus laugh?
Ten tickles.

What is stranger than seeing a catfish?

Seeing a fishbowl.

What kind of fish are made for freezing weather?
Skates.

What does a fish hang on its door at Christmas?
A coral wreath.

Why is it so easy to weigh fish?
Because they have their own scales.

What animals are found on legal documents?

Seals.

Where does seafood shop?
At the fish market.

What is a knight's favorite food?
Swordfish.

What is the ocean's best subject?
   Current events.

What washes up on tiny beaches?
   Microwaves.

How can you tell that the ocean is friendly?
   It waves.

How does a fish feel when it is caught stealing bait?
   Gillty.

What keeps the ocean clean?
   Tide with beach.

Where does bacon go on vacation?
   The Pigcific Ocean.

If the earth were flat and a fish swam over the edge, where would it go?

Trouter space.

What is the most affectionate animal in the sea?

A cuddlefish.

Why did the fish cross the ocean?

To get to the other tide.

What is green and has a trunk?

A seasick tourist.

What do you call two octopuses that look alike?

Itentacle twins.

What should you do if you are stranded on an iceberg?
    Just chill.

Why is the letter T
like an island?

Because it's in the middle of water.

Why do fish live in salt water?
    Because pepper makes them sneeze.

What did the beach say when the tide came in?
    "Long time no sea."

Where do sea cows sleep at night?
In the barnacle.

What do you call a snail on a ship?
A snailor.

How did the fish cross the pond?
Very effishently.

Why did the sailor sell things on his ship?
It wouldn't go without a sale.

How does a mermaid call a friend?
On her shell phone.

Where did the whale play his violin?
In the orcastra.

What building is easy to lift?

A lighthouse.

Goofy Games

What is the quietest game in the world?
Bowling—you can hear a pin drop.

What do you call a boomerang that doesn't come back to you?
A bummerang.

Why was the piano tuner hired to play on the baseball team?
Because he had perfect pitch.

What is a frog's favorite game?
Croaket.

What do championship football players eat their cereal in?

Super bowls.

What is a pig's favorite position in baseball?

Snortstop.

Why was the baseball player invited to go on the camping trip?

To pitch the tent.

Why do porcupines never lose games?

Because they always have the most points.

What did the King of Hearts say to the King of Spades?

"Let's make a deal."

Why couldn't the chicken get on base?
Because she kept hitting fowl balls.

What did the umpire say to the car?
"Steer-ike one!"

Why did the golfer wear two pairs of pants?
In case he got a hole in one.

What is a hand's favorite sport?
Finger skating.

What do you call a fly with no wings?
A walk.

What is a snowman's favorite game?
Freezebee.

Why is Cinderella so bad at sports?
Because she has a pumpkin for a coach and runs away from the ball.

What baseball team does a jokester like best?
The New York Prankees.

What can you serve but not eat?

A tennis ball.

What is the first thing a ball does when it
stops rolling?
It looks round.

What do you call a yo-yo without string?
A no-yo.

Which game do fish like to play?
Salmon Says.

Which baseball team do puppies play for?
The New York Pets.

What has four legs and catches flies?
Two outfielders.

What do you call four bullfighters in quicksand?
Cuatro sinko.

What is a ghost's favorite position in soccer?
Ghoulkeeper.

What is a cheerleader's favorite color?
Yeller.

When is a baby good at basketball?
When it's dribbling.

Why did the basketball player go to jail?
Because he shot the ball.

When do basketball players love doughnuts?
When they dunk them.

What do you call a pig that plays basketball?
A ball hog.

How is a baseball team like a pancake?
They both need a good batter.

What's a golfer's favorite letter?
T.

What animal is best at hitting a baseball?
A bat.

Why do frogs make
good outfielders?

Because they never miss a fly.

What is a waiter's favorite sport?
Tennis, because he serves so well.

Why did the football coach go to the bank?
He wanted his quarterback.

Why is tennis such a loud sport?
The players raise a racket.

Why did Tarzan spend so much time on the golf course?
He was perfecting his swing.

Why did the ballerina quit?
Because it was tutu hard.

What is an insect's favorite sport?
Cricket.

How do basketball players stay cool during the game?

They stand close to the fans.

What do hockey players and magicians have in common?

Both do hat tricks.

What type of drink do football players hate?

Penaltea.

Why was the man doing the backstroke?

He didn't want to swim on a full stomach.

What is the hardest part about skydiving?

The ground.

What's the best part of a boxer's joke?

The punch line.

What is a basketball player's favorite cheese?
  Swish.

What is a tornado's favorite game?
  Twister.

What do you call a pig that knows karate?

  A pork chop.

What do you call a spoiled tightrope walker?
  An acrobrat.

What did the cat say when it struck out at the baseball game?

"*Me-out?*"

Why did the baseball bat go to the recording studio?

To get a big hit.

Grins in Gear

Why couldn't the bicycle stand up by itself?
It was two tired.

What kind of car has whiskers and purrs?

A Catillac.

Where do cars go swimming?
In a carpool.

Where do race cars go to wash their clothes?
The laundry vroom.

What kind of train needs a hankie?
An ah-choo-choo train.

What kind of bus has two floors and says,
"Quack"?
A double ducker.

How do snowmen travel around?
By icicle.

Where would a car go after an accident?
To an accidentist.

Why did the traffic light turn red?
You would, too, if you had to change in the middle of the street.

Where would a car go on vacation?
To Key West.

What did the tire say to the truck driver?
"Give me a brake!"

How can you drive two thousand miles with a flat tire?

Your spare tire is flat—the four you're riding on are fine.

How does a rose ride a bike?
By pushing its petals.

Two wrongs do not make a right. But what do two rights make?
The first airplane.

What is a car's favorite place to dine?
The gas station.

What does a car wear on its head?
A gas cap.

What is black and white with a cherry on top?
A police car.

What gives milk and has a horn?
A milk truck.

What would happen if all the cars in the country were painted pink?

It would be a pink car nation.

What do you get if you cross a bird, a car, and a dog?

A flying carpet.

How can you tell a motorcyclist is happy?

By the number of bugs in his teeth.

What is a song about a car called?

A car tune.

How do rabbits travel?

By hareplane.

How do you top a car?
You 'tep on the brake.

Why are police officers the strongest people in the world?

Because they can hold up traffic with one hand.

What goes best with a white wall?
  A hubcap.

How do stairs travel?
  By flight.

What do you call the life story of a car?
  An autobiography.

What has four wheels and flies?
  A garbage truck.

How did the locomotive learn to run on tracks?
  It trained for it.

What did the traffic light say to the car?
  "Don't look—I'm changing."

What do you call a Spanish knight with a rotary engine?

Don Quixote de la Mazda.

What do you call a bike when it blows a tire?

A popcycle.

What happened to the frog that parked illegally?

He got toad.

What did the car wheels say after a long drive?

"We're tired out!"

Wacky Weather

What's the difference between a horse and the weather?

One is reined up and the other rains down.

What did one tornado say to the other?

"Let's twist again like we did last summer."

What happens when it rains cats and dogs?

You have to be careful not to step in a poodle.

What do you call it when it rains chickens and ducks?

Fowl weather.

What's the difference between weather and climate?

You can't weather a tree, but you can climate.

Why did Jennifer go outside with her purse open?

She was expecting some change in the weather.

What did one hurricane say to the other?

"I have my eye on you."

How do you find out the weather when you're on vacation?
Look out the window.

What does a cloud wear under its raincoat?
Thunderwear.

What do clouds wear in their hair?
Rainbows.

What happens when the fog lifts in California?
UCLA.

What happened to the wind?
It blew away.

What do you call a snowman with sharp teeth?
Frostbite.

What is the coldest month of the year?
Decembrrrrrr.

What did summer say to spring?
Help—I'm going to fall!

What do you get when you cross a bear with
a rain cloud?
A drizzly bear.

Why should you never tell a joke while ice fishing?
Because the ice will crack up.

What did the raindrop say when it fell?
"Oops—I dripped!"

What is worse than raining cats and dogs?

Hailing taxis.

What did one snowman say to the other?
"Is it me, or do you smell carrots?"

What is a snowman's favorite lunch?
An iceberger.

What happened when the snowwoman got angry at the snowman?

She gave him the cold shoulder.

Where do snowpeople dance?
  At a snowball.

What do snowmen wear on their heads?
  Ice caps.

Grab Bag

Why are pine trees such bad knitters?
They are always dropping their needles.

In which month did the Puritans come to America?
April. April showers bring Mayflowers.

Can February March?
No, but April May.

Why is everyone so tired on April 1?
Because they just had a thirty-one-day March.

Why did Humpty Dumpty have a great fall?
To make up for a miserable summer.

Why is your nose in the middle of your face?

Because it's the scenter.

What two keys cannot open any doors?
A donkey and a monkey.

What do you get when you cross a dog with an elephant?

A very nervous mailman.

Why did the woman put lipstick on her forehead?
To make up her mind.

What's green and makes holes?
A drill pickle.

Why did Sunday beat Monday in a boxing match?
Because Monday was a weak day.

What did Cinderella say when her pictures didn't arrive?
"Someday my prints will come."

How do you hurt a joke?
By giving it a punch line.

Where do polar bears vote?

The North Poll.

What did the shirt button say to his neighbor?
"Help! I'm hanging on by a thread!"

How do billboards talk?
They use sign language.

What do ambitious young rabbits want to be when they grow up?

Millionhares.

How do angels greet people?
"Halo."

What do mallards
hang up for
the holidays?

Duckorations.

How did the sledgehammer do in the talent show?
   She was a smashing success.

What color are books you've finished?
   Red.

What did one penny say to the other?
   "It makes cents to work together."

What do you call a hawk that can draw and play the guitar?

Talonted.

When is a mailbox like the alphabet?

When it's full of letters.

What did the paper clip say to the magnet?
   "You're so attractive!"

What is the rudest bird?

A mockingbird.

Why did the dinosaur cross the road?

Because chickens weren't invented yet.

Why wouldn't the grizzly walk on a gravel road?

It had bear feet.

What does a cow use to cut grass?

A lawnmooer.

What is the quickest way to double your money?
Fold it in half.

What is a volcano?
A mountain with hiccups.

What has wheels and a trunk, but no engine?

An elephant on roller skates.